Against All Odds
A Journey in Scripture from
A to Z

Man shall not live by bread alone, but by every word that proceeds from the mouth of God. Matthew 4:4

Against All Odds Scriptural Journal

This Journal Belongs To:

_____

Date:

_____

From:

_____

Against All Odds
Table of Contents

Contact Information:
Pastor Lauren Denise Carpenter
Church Website: www.thefaithchurchministries.com
Facebook: www.facebook.com/LDeniseCarpenter
Twitter: www.twitter/com/PastorDenise7
Email: AAObook1@gmail.com

Journal Cover Design: Derrick Carpenter Jr.
Journal Editor: Jasmine Carpenter-Elliott

All Reference Scriptures are from King James and New King James Versions

I pray the Against All Odds Journal will help spark and motivate you to read God's Word on a daily basis. Blessings to you and your family.

~Pastor Lauren Denise Carpenter

Ask and ye shall receive, seek and ye shall find, knock and the door shall be open unto you.
Luke 11:9

_____

_____

_____

_____

_____

But my God shall supply all your needs according to His riches in glory by Christ Jesus. Philippians 4:19

_____

_____

_____

_____

_____

Casting all your cares upon Him for He cares for you.
1 Peter 5:7

_____

_____

_____

_____

_____

_____

Delight thyself in the Lord and He shall give you the desires of your heart. Psalms 37:4

_____

_____

_____

_____

_____

_____

Every good and every perfect gift comes from above and from the Father of light.
James 1:17

_____

_____

_____

_____

_____

For we walk by faith and not by sight. 2 Corinthians 5:7

_____

_____

_____

_____

_____

_____

God has not given us the spirit of fear, but of power and of love and of a sound mind.
2 Timothy 1:7

_____

_____

_____

_____

_____

_____

He that dwells in the secret place of the most high shall abide under the shadow of the almighty. Psalms 91:1

_____

_____

_____

_____

_____

I can do all things through Christ that strengthens me. Philippians 4:13

_____

_____

_____

_____

_____

_____

Joy of the Lord is my strength. Nehemiah 8:10

_____

_____

_____

_____

_____

_____

_____

Know ye not that your body is the temple of the Holy Ghost.
1 Corinthians 6:19

_____

_____

_____

_____

_____

_____

Looking unto Jesus the author and the finisher of our faith. Hebrews 12:2

_____

_____

_____

_____

_____

_____

Many are the afflictions of the righteous, but the Lord delivers him out of them all. Psalms 34:19

_____

_____

_____

_____

_____

No weapon formed against me shall prosper.
Isaiah 54:17

_____

_____

_____

_____

_____

_____

Obedience is better than sacrifice. 1 Samuel 15:22

_____

_____

_____

_____

_____

_____

_____

Put on the whole armor of God that you may be able to stand against the wiles of the devil.
Ephesians 6:11

_____

_____

_____

_____

_____

_____

Quench not the spirit of God.

1 Thessalonians 5:19

_____

_____

_____

_____

_____

_____

_____

Rejoice in the Lord always again I say rejoice.
Philippians 4:4

_____

_____

_____

_____

_____

_____

Seek ye first the kingdom of God and His righteousness and all these things shall be added unto you. Matthew 6:33

_____

_____

_____

_____

_____

_____

They that wait upon the Lord, shall renew their strength. Isaiah 40:31

_____

_____

_____

_____

_____

_____

Unto us a child is born in the city of David. Luke 2:11

_____

_____

_____

_____

_____

_____

_____

Verily, verily I say unto you, except a man be born again, he shall not see the kingdom of God.
John 3:3

_____

_____

_____

_____

_____

_____

What things soever you desire when you pray, believe that you will receive them and you shall have them. Mark 11:24

_____

_____

_____

_____

_____

Except a man be born again, he shall not see the kingdom of God. John 3:3

_____

_____

_____

_____

_____

_____

Yield ye your members as instruments of righteousness unto God. Romans 6:13

_____

_____

_____

_____

_____

_____

Zaccheus make haste and come down; for today I must abide at thy house. Luke 19:5

_____

_____

_____

_____

_____

_____

Man shall not live by bread alone, but by every word that proceeds from the mouth of God. Matthew 4:4

As I experienced the odds against me, God's Word brought me Victory from A-Z

From Anger to Attitude

Proverbs 16:32 -He who is slow to anger is better than the mighty, and he who rules his spirit than he who takes a city.

Proverbs 17:22 -A merry heart does good, like medicine, But a broken spirit dries the bones.

Proverbs 15:13 -A merry heart makes a cheerful countenance, But by sorrow of the heart the spirit is broken.

From Abortion to Abundance

Exodus20:13 -You shall not murder.

Psalm 106:37-38 -They even sacrificed their sons And

their daughters to demons, And shed innocent blood, The blood of their sons and daughters, Whom they sacrificed to the idols of Canaan; And the land was polluted with blood.

Psalm 92:12 -The righteous shall flourish like a palm tree, He shall grow like a cedar in Lebanon.

Deuteronomy 30:9-10 -The Lord your God will make you abound in all the work of your hand, in the fruit of your body, in the increase of your livestock, and in the produce of your land for good. For the Lord will again rejoice over you for good as He rejoiced over your fathers, if you obey the voice of the Lord your God, to keep his commandments and His statues which are written in this Book of the Law, and if you turn to the Lord your God with all your heart and with all your soul.

From Abuse to Access

Psalm 56:11 -In God I have put my trust; I will not be afraid. What can man do to me?

Proverbs 18:24 -A man who has friends must himself be

friendly, But there is a friend who sticks closer than a brother.

Ephesians 2:18 -For through Him we both have access by one Spirit to the Father.

From Addiction to Achievement

Psalm 107:20 -He sent His word and healed them, and delivered them from their destructions.

Philippians 4:13 -I can do all things through Christ who strengthens me.

Isaiah 59:1 -Behold, the Lord's hand is not shortened, that it cannot save; nor His ear heavy, that it cannot hear.

John 8:32 -And you shall know the truth, and the truth shall make you free.

Mark 11:24 -Therefore I say to you, whatever things you ask when you pray, believe that you receive them, and you will have them.

Psalm 2:8 -Ask of Me, and I will give you the nations for your inheritance, and the ends of the earth for your possession.

From Betrayal to Boldness

Genesis 50:20 -But as for you, you meant evil against me; but God meant it for good, in order to bring it about as it is this day, to save many people alive.

Psalm 41:9-10 -Even my own familiar friend in whom I trusted, who ate my bread, has lifted up his heel against me. But You, O Lord, be merciful to me, and raise me up, that I may repay them.

Acts 1:8 -But you shall receive power when the Holy Spirit has come upon you; and you shall be witnesses to Me in Jerusalem, and in all Judea and Samaria, and to the end of the earth.

Acts 18:9-10 -Now the Lord spoke to Paul in the night by a vision, "Do not be afraid, but speak, and do not keep silent; 10 for I am with you, and no one will attack you to hurt you; for I have many people in this city."

From Bitter to Better

Ephesians 4:26-32 -"Be angry, and do not sin": do not let the sun go down on your wrath, 27 nor give place to the devil. 28 Let him who stole steal no longer, but rather let him labor, working with his hands what is good, that he may have something to give him who has need. 29 Let no corrupt word proceed out of your mouth, but what is good for necessary edification, that it may impart grace to the hearers. 30 And do not grieve the Holy Spirit of God, by whom you were sealed for the day of redemption. 31 Let all bitterness, wrath, anger, clamor, and evil speaking be put away from you, with all malice. 32 And be kind to one another, tenderhearted, forgiving one another, even as God in Christ forgave you.

From Bitterness to Blessings

Proverbs 14:10 -The heart knows its own bitterness, and a stranger does not share its joy.

Hebrews 12:14-15 -Pursue peace with all people, and holiness, without which no one will see the Lord: 15 looking carefully lest anyone fall short of the grace of God; lest any root of bitterness springing up cause trouble, and by this many become defiled.

Genesis 12:2 -I will make you a great nation; I will bless you. And make your name great; and you shall be a blessing.

Deuteronomy 28:2 -And all these blessings shall come upon you and overtake you, because you obey the voice of the Lord your God.

From Crisis to Courage

Psalm 23:4 -Yea, though I walk through the valley of the shadow of death, I will fear no evil; For You are with me; your rod and Your staff, they comfort me.

Psalm 46:1-3 -God is our refuge and strength, a very present help in trouble. 2 Therefore we will not fear, Even though the earth be removed, And though the mountains be carried into the midst of the sea; 3 Though its waters roar and be troubled, Though the mountains shake with its swelling. Selah

Deuteronomy 31:6 -Be strong and of good courage, do not fear nor be afraid of them; for the Lord your God, He is the One who goes with you. He will not leave you nor forsake you.

Psalm 31:24 -Be of good courage, And He shall strengthen your heart, all you who hope in the Lord.

From Complaining to Compassion

Philippians 4:11 -Not that I speak in regard to need, for I have learned in whatever state I am, to be content.

Philippians 2:14 -Do all things without complaining and disputing.

Isaiah 49:15 -"Can a woman forget her nursing child, and not have compassion on the son of her womb? Surely they may forget, yet I will not forget you.

Psalm 78:38 -But He, being full of compassion, forgave their iniquity, and did not destroy them. Yes, many a time He turned His anger away, and did not stir up all His wrath.

From Depression to Deliverance

Psalm 30:5 -For His anger is but for a moment, His favor is for life;

Weeping may endure for a night, but joy comes in the morning.

Proverbs 13:12 -Hope deferred makes the heart sick, But when the desire comes, it is a tree of life.

Psalm 31:2 -Bow down Your ear to me, Deliver me speedily; be my rock of refuge, a fortress of defense to save me.

Psalm 34:4 -I sought the Lord, and He heard me, and delivered me from all my fears.

From Doubts to Dreams

Mark 11:23 -For assuredly, I say to you, whoever says to this mountain, 'Be removed and be cast into the sea,' and does not doubt in his heart, but believes that those things he says will be done, he will have whatever he says.

James 1:6 -But let him ask in faith, with no doubting, for he who doubts is like a wave of the sea driven and tossed by the wind.

Joel 2:28 -"And it shall come to pass afterward That I will pour out My Spirit on all flesh; Your sons and your daughters shall prophesy, Your old men shall dream dreams, Your young men shall see visions.

Job 33:14-17 -For God may speak in one way, or in another, yet man does not perceive it. 15 In a dream, in a vision of the night, when deep sleep falls upon men, while slumbering on their beds, 16 Then He opens the ears of men, And seals their instruction. 17 In order to turn man from his deed, and conceal pride from man.

From Enemies to Endurance

Psalm 119:98 -You, through Your commandments, make me wiser than my enemies; For they are ever with me.

Matthew 5:44 -But I say to you, love your enemies, bless those who curse you, do good to those who hate you, and pray for those who spitefully use you and persecute you.

Galatians 6:9 -And let us not grow weary while doing good, for in due season we shall reap if we do not lose heart.

Revelation 21:7 -He who overcomes shall inherit all

things, and I will be his God and he shall be My son.

From Envy to Excellence

Proverbs 27:4 -Wrath is cruel and anger a torrent, But who is able to stand before jealousy?

1 Peter 2:1 -Therefore, laying aside all malice, all deceit, hypocrisy, envy, and all evil speaking.

Proverbs 17:27 -He who has knowledge spares his words, And a man of understanding is of a calm spirit.

Proverbs 8:6 -Listen, for I will speak of excellent things, And from the opening of my lips will come right things.

From Fear to Faith

2 Timothy 1:7 -For God has not given us a spirit of fear, but of power and of love and of a sound mind.

Hebrews 13:6 -So we may boldly say: "The Lord is my helper; I will not fear. What can man do to me?"

2 Corinthians 5:7 -For we walk by faith, not by sight.

Hebrew 11:6 -But without faith it is impossible to please Him, for he who comes to God must believe that He is, and that He is a rewarder of those who diligently seek Him.

From Failure to Favor

Galatians 6:1-2 -Brethren, if a man is overtaken in any trespass, you who are spiritual restore such a one in a spirit of gentleness, considering yourself lest you also be tempted. 2 Bear one another's burdens, and so fulfill the law of Christ.

Proverbs 24:16 -For a righteous man may fall seven times And rise again, But the wicked shall fall by calamity.

Proverbs 12:2 -A good man obtains favor from the Lord, But a man of wicked intentions He will condemn.

Proverbs 22:1 -A good name is to be chosen rather than great riches, Loving favor rather than silver and gold.

From Grief to Growth

Psalm 30:5 -For His anger is but for a moment, His favor is for life; Weeping may endure for a night, But joy comes in the morning.

Matthew 5:4 -Blessed are those who mourn, For they shall be comforted.

Isaiah 43:18-19 -"Do not remember the former things, Nor consider the things of old. 19 Behold, I will do a new thing, Now it shall spring forth; Shall you not know it? I will even make a road in the wilderness, And rivers in the desert.

From Guilt to Guidance

Isaiah 1:18 -"Come now, and let us reason together," Says the Lord, "Though your sins are like scarlet, They shall be as white as snow; Though they are red like crimson, They shall be as wool.

Romans 8:1 -There is therefore now no condemnation to those who are in Christ Jesus, who do not walk according to the flesh, but according to the Spirit.

Psalm 31:3 -For You are my rock and my fortress; Therefore, for Your name's sake, Lead me and guide me.

Psalm 32:8 -I will instruct you and teach you in the way you should go; I will guide you with My eye.

Jeremiah 3:4 -Will you not from this time cry to Me,
'My Father, You are the guide of my youth?

1 John 1:9 -If we confess our sins, He is faithful and just
to forgive us our sins and to cleanse us from all
unrighteousness.

From Greed to Gratitude

Psalm 100:4 -Enter into His gates with thanksgiving,
And into His courts with praise. Be thankful to Him, and
bless His name.

Psalm 92:1 -It is good to give thanks to the Lord, And to
sing praises to Your name, O Most High.

I Thessalonians 5:18 -In everything give thanks; for this
is the will of God in Christ Jesus for you.

From Heartache to Healing

Psalm 34:18 -The Lord is near to those who have a
broken heart, And saves such as have a contrite spirit.

Proverbs 12:25 -Anxiety in the heart of man causes

depression, But a good word makes it glad.

Psalm 103:2-3 -Bless the Lord, O my soul, And forget not all His benefits: 3 Who forgives all your iniquities, Who heals all your diseases.

Jeremiah 30:17 -For I will restore health to you And heal you of your wounds, says the Lord, 'Because they called you an outcast saying: "This is Zion; No one seeks her."'

Psalm 147:3 -He heals the brokenhearted And binds up their wounds.

3 John 1:2 -Beloved, I pray that you may prosper in all things and be in health, just as your soul prospers.

From Hurt to Hope

Isaiah 54:17 -No weapon formed against you shall prosper, And every tongue which rises against you in judgment You shall condemn. This is the heritage of the servants of the Lord, And their righteousness is from Me," Says the Lord.

2 Timothy 4:18 -And the Lord will deliver me from

every evil work and preserve me for His heavenly kingdom. To Him be glory forever and ever. Amen!

Psalm 33:18 -Behold, the eye of the Lord is on those who fear Him, On those who hope in His mercy.

Psalm 71:5 -For You are my hope, O Lord God; You are my trust from my youth.

From Impatience to Increase

Psalm 27:14 -Wait on the Lord; Be of good courage, And He shall strengthen your heart; Wait, I say, on the Lord!

James 1:4 -But let patience have its perfect work, that you may be perfect and complete, lacking nothing.

1 Thessalonians 3:12 -And may the Lord make you increase and abound in love to one another and to all, just as we do to you

2 Corinthians -Now may He who supplies seed to the sower, and bread for food, supply and multiply the seed you have sown and increase the fruits of your righteousness.

From Jealousy to Joy

Song of Solomon 8:6 -Set me as a seal upon your heart, As a seal upon your arm; For love is as strong as death, Jealousy as cruel as the grave; Its flames are flames of fire, A most vehement flame.

Exodus 20:17 -"You shall not covet your neighbor's house; you shall not covet your neighbor's wife, nor his male servant, nor his female servant, nor his ox, nor his donkey, nor anything that is your neighbor's."

Ecclesiastes 4:4 -Again, I saw that for all toil and every skillful work a man is envied by his neighbor. This also is vanity and grasping for the wind.

Nehemiah 8:10 -Then he said to them, "Go your way, eat the fat, drink the sweet, and send portions to those for whom nothing is prepared; for this day is holy to our Lord. Do not sorrow, for the joy of the Lord is your strength."

Psalm 5:11 -But let all those rejoice who put their trust in You; Let them ever shout for joy, because You defend them; Let those also who love Your name Be joyful in You.

From Killing to Kindness

Psalm 117:2 -For His merciful kindness is great toward us, And the truth of the Lord endures forever. Praise the Lord!

1 Corinthians 13:4 -Love suffers long and is kind; love does not envy; love does not parade itself, is not puffed up.

Ephesians 4:32 -And be kind to one another, tenderhearted, forgiving one another, even as God in Christ forgave you.

From Lost to Life

Joel 2:25 -"So I will restore to you the years that the swarming locust has eaten, The crawling locust, The consuming locust, And the chewing locust, My great army which I sent among you.

John 10:10 -The thief does not come except to steal, and to kill, and to destroy. I have come that they may have life, and that they may have it more abundantly.

Proverbs 4:20-22 -My son, give attention to my words; Incline your ear to my sayings. 21 Do not let them depart from your eyes; Keep them in the midst of your heart; 22 For they are life to those who find them, And health to all their flesh.

Proverbs 8:35 -For whoever finds me finds life, And obtains favor from the Lord.

Colossians 3:4 -When Christ who is our life appears, then you also will appear with Him in glory.

From Lust to Love

James 1:13-14 -Let no one say when he is tempted, "I am tempted by God"; for God cannot be tempted by evil, nor does He Himself tempt anyone. 14 But each one is tempted when he is drawn away by his own desires and enticed.

Ephesians 4:22-24 -That you put off, concerning your former conduct, the old man which grows corrupt according to the deceitful lusts, 23 and be renewed in the spirit of your mind, 24 and that you put on the new man which was created according to God, in true righteousness and holiness.

John 3:16 -For God so loved the world that He gave His only begotten Son, that whoever believes in Him should not perish but have everlasting life.

John 13:34-35 -A new commandment I give to you, that you love one another; as I have loved you, that you also love one another. 35 By this all will know that you are My disciples, if you have love for one another."

Romans 5:5 -Now hope does not disappoint, because the love of God has been poured out in our hearts by the Holy Spirit who was given to us.

From Laziness to Loyalty

Proverbs 12:24 -The hand of the diligent will rule, But the lazy man will be put to forced labor.

Proverbs 13:4 -The soul of a lazy man desires, and has nothing; But the soul of the diligent shall be made rich.

Ecclesiastes 9:10 -Whatever your hand finds to do, do it with your might; for there is no work or device or knowledge or wisdom in the grave where you are going.

Proverbs 28:20 -A faithful man will abound with blessings, But he who hastens to be rich will not go unpunished.

Proverbs 25: 15 -By long forbearance a ruler is persuaded, And a gentle tongue breaks a bone.

From Mess to Miracles

Proverbs 24:16 -For a righteous man may fall seven times And rise again, But the wicked shall fall by calamity.

Acts 10:38 -How God anointed Jesus of Nazareth with the Holy Spirit and with power, who went about doing good and healing all who were oppressed by the devil, for God was with Him.

Jeremiah 32:17 -Ah, Lord God! Behold, You have made

the heavens and the earth by Your great power and outstretched arm. There is nothing too hard for You.

From Moods to Memories

Proverbs 15:13 -A merry heart makes a cheerful countenance, But by sorrow of the heart the spirit is broken.

Proverbs 15:15-All the days of the afflicted are evil, But he who is of a merry heart has a continual feast.

Proverbs 17:22 -A merry heart does good, like medicine, But a broken spirit dries the bones.

Proverbs 21:19 -Better to dwell in the wilderness, Than with a contentious and angry woman.

II Timothy 3:15 -And that from childhood you have known the Holy Scriptures, which are able to make you wise for salvation through faith which is in Christ Jesus.

Psalm 119:11 -Your word I have hidden in my heart, That I might not sin against You.

Deuteronomy 6:7-9 -7 You shall teach them diligently to your children, and shall talk of them when you sit in your house, when you walk by the way, when you lie down, and when you rise up. 8 You shall bind them as a sign on your hand, and they shall be as frontlets between your eyes. 9 You shall write them on the doorposts of your house and on your gates.

From Mistake to Mercy

Psalm 37: 23-24 -The steps of a good man are ordered by the Lord, And He delights in his way. 24 Though he fall, he shall not be utterly cast down; For the Lord upholds him with His hand.

Proverbs 24:16 -For a righteous man may fall seven times And rise again, But the wicked shall fall by calamity.

Isaiah 1:18 -"Come now, and let us reason together," Says the Lord, "Though your sins are like scarlet, They shall be as white as snow; Though they are red like crimson, They shall be as wool.

Psalm 86:5 -For You, Lord, are good, and ready to forgive, And abundant in mercy to all those who call upon You.

Psalm 103:8 -The Lord is merciful and gracious, Slow to anger, and abounding in mercy.

Matthew 5:7 -Blessed are the merciful, For they shall obtain mercy.

From Never to New

Hebrews 10:11 -11And every priest stands ministering daily and offering repeatedly the same sacrifices, which can never take away sins.

Isaiah 43:19 -Behold, I will do a new thing, Now it shall spring forth; Shall you not know it? I will even make a road in the wilderness And rivers in the desert.

II Corinthians 5:17 -Therefore, if anyone is in Christ, he is a new creation; old things have passed away; behold, all things have become new.

Revelation 21:5 -Then He who sat on the throne said,

"Behold, I make all things new." And He said to me, "Write, for these words are true and faithful."

From No to Negotiate

Proverbs 15:1 -A soft answer turns away wrath, But a harsh word stirs up anger.

Isaiah 54:17 -No weapon formed against you shall prosper, And every tongue which rises against you in judgment You shall condemn. This is the heritage of the servants of the Lord, And their righteousness is from Me," Says the LORD.

Matthew 5:41 -And whoever compels you to go one mile, go with him two.

Proverbs 16:24 -Pleasant words are like a honeycomb, Sweetness to the soul and health to the bones.

From Offenses to Obedience

Exodus 23: 22-23 -22 But if you indeed obey His voice and do all that I speak, then I will be an enemy to your enemies and an adversary to your adversaries. 23 For My

Angel will go before you and bring you in to the Amorites and the Hittites and the Perizzites and the Canaanites and the Hivites and the Jebusites; and I will cut them off.

I Samuel 15:22-So Samuel said: "Has the Lord as great delight in burnt offerings and sacrifices, As in obeying the voice of the Lord? Behold, to obey is better than sacrifice, And to heed than the fat of rams.

I John 2:3 -3 Now by this we know that we know Him, if we keep His commandments.

Isaiah 1:19 -If you are willing and obedient, You shall eat the good of the land.

I John 3:22 -And whatever we ask we receive from Him, because we keep His commandments and do those things that are pleasing in His sight.

From Overload to Overcoming

Romans 12:1 -I beseech you therefore, brethren, by the mercies of God, that you present your bodies a living sacrifice, holy, acceptable to God, which is your reasonable service.

Romans 2:7 -Eternal life to those who by patient continuance in doing good seek for glory, honor, and immortality.

I John 4:4 -You are of God, little children, and have overcome them, because He who is in you is greater than he who is in the world.

Revelation 2:7 -"He who has an ear, let him hear what the Spirit says to the churches. To him who overcomes I will give to eat from the tree of life, which is in the midst of the Paradise of God."'

Revelation 3:21 -To him who overcomes I will grant to sit with Me on My throne, as I also overcame and sat down with My Father on His throne.

From Problems to Promotion

Proverbs 3:35 -The wise shall inherit glory, But shame shall be the legacy of fools.

Psalm 147:3 -He heals the brokenhearted And binds up

their wounds.

Psalm 75:6-7 - 6 For exaltation comes neither from the east Nor from the west nor from the south. 7 But God is the Judge: He puts down one, And exalts another.

Philippians 3:14 -I press toward the goal for the prize of the upward call of God in Christ Jesus.

From Pain to Praise

Psalm 34:19 -Many are the afflictions of the righteous, But the Lord delivers him out of them all.

Revelation 21:4 -And God will wipe away every tear from their eyes; there shall be no more death, nor sorrow, nor crying. There shall be no more pain, for the former things have passed away.

Psalm 34:1 -I will bless the Lord at all times; His praise shall continually be in my mouth.

Psalm 149:3 -Let them praise His name with the dance; Let them sing praises to Him with the timbrel and harp.

Psalm 150 -1 Praise the LORD! Praise God in His sanctuary; Praise Him in His mighty firmament! 2 Praise Him for His mighty acts; Praise Him according to His excellent greatness! 3 Praise Him with the sound of the trumpet; Praise Him with the lute and harp! 4 Praise Him with the timbrel and dance; Praise Him with stringed instruments and flutes! 5 Praise Him with loud cymbals; Praise Him with clashing cymbals! 6 Let everything that has breath praise the Lord. Praise the Lord!

Psalm 69:30 -I will praise the name of God with a song, And will magnify Him with thanksgiving.

From Pride to Prayer

Proverbs 11:2 -When pride comes, then comes shame; But with the humble is wisdom.

Proverbs 16: 18-19 -Pride goes before destruction, And a haughty spirit before a fall. 19 Better to be of a humble spirit with the lowly, Than to divide the spoil with the proud.

James 4:6 -But He gives more grace. Therefore He says: "God resists the proud, But gives grace to the humble."

Colossians 4:2 -Continue earnestly in prayer, being vigilant in it with thanksgiving.

I Thessalonians 5:17 -Pray without ceasing.

I Chronicles 16:11 -Seek the Lord and His strength; Seek His face evermore!

James 5:16 -Confess your trespasses to one another, and pray for one another, that you may be healed. The effective, fervent prayer of a righteous man avails much.

From Pitfalls to Power

Psalm 91:3 -Surely He shall deliver you from the snare of the fowler And from the perilous pestilence.

Psalm 119:110 -The wicked have laid a snare for me, Yet I have not strayed from Your precepts.

Acts 1:8 -But you shall receive power when the Holy Spirit has come upon you; and you shall be witnesses to Me in Jerusalem, and in all Judea and Samaria, and to the end of the earth.

Matthew 28:18 -And Jesus came and spoke to them, saying, "All authority has been given to Me in heaven and on earth.

Proverbs 18:21 -Death and life are in the power of the tongue, And those who love it will eat its fruit.

From Quit to Quite

Deuteronomy 31:6 -Be strong and of good courage, do not fear nor be afraid of them; for the Lord your God, He is the One who goes with you. He will not leave you nor forsake you."

Matthew 10:22 -And you will be hated by all for My name's sake. But he who endures to the end will be saved.

Luke 9:62 -But Jesus said to him, "No one, having put his hand to the plow, and looking back, is fit for the kingdom of God."

II Timothy 2:3 -You therefore must endure hardship as a good soldier of Jesus Christ.

Revelation 21:23 -The city had no need of the sun or of the moon to shine in it, for the glory of God illuminated it. The Lamb is its light.

I Thessalonians 4:11 -That you also aspire to lead a quiet life, to mind your own business, and to work with your own hands, as we commanded you.

Ecclesiastes 3:7 -A time to tear, And a time to sew; A time to keep silence, And a time to speak.

Ecclesiastes 4:6 -Better a handful with quietness Than both hands full, together with toil and grasping for the wind.

From Repentance to Restoration

I John 1:9 -If we confess our sins, He is faithful and just to forgive us our sins and to cleanse us from all unrighteousness.

II Peter 3:9 -The Lord is not slack concerning His promise, as some count slackness, but is longsuffering toward us, not willing that any should perish but that all should come to repentance.

Acts 17:30 -Truly, these times of ignorance God overlooked, but now commands all men everywhere to repent.

From Regret to Respect

Philippians 3:13 -Brethren, I do not count myself to have apprehended; but one thing I do, forgetting those things which are behind and reaching forward to those things which are ahead.

Psalm 38:18 -For I will declare my iniquity; I will be in anguish over my sin.

Proverbs 22:1 -A good name is to be chosen rather than great riches, Loving favor rather than silver and gold.

Numbers 27:18-20 -18And the Lord said to Moses: "Take Joshua the son of Nun with you, a man in whom is the Spirit, and lay your hand on him; 19 set him before Eleazar the priest and before all the congregation, and inaugurate him in their sight. 20 And you shall give some of your authority to him, that all the congregation of the children of Israel may be obedient.

From Rejection to Reputation

Psalm 27:10 -When my father and my mother forsake me, Then the Lord will take care of me.

Isaiah 53:3 -He is despised and rejected by men, A Man of sorrows and acquainted with grief. And we hid, as it were, our faces from Him; He was despised, and we did not esteem Him.

Matthew 4:24 -Then His fame went throughout all Syria; and they brought to Him all sick people who were afflicted with various diseases and torments, and those who were demon-possessed, epileptics, and paralytics; and He healed them.

Matthew 5:16 -Let your light so shine before men, that they may see your good works and glorify your Father in heaven.

Proverbs 22:1 -A good name is to be chosen rather than great riches, Loving favor rather than silver and gold.

From Stress to Strength

I Peter 5:7 -Casting all your care upon Him, for He cares for you.

Psalm 73:26 -My flesh and my heart fail; But God is the strength of my heart and my portion forever.

Proverbs 24:5 -A wise man is strong, Yes, a man of knowledge increases strength.

Nehemiah 8:10 -Then he said to them, "Go your way, eat the fat, drink the sweet, and send portions to those for whom nothing is prepared; for this day is holy to our Lord. Do not sorrow, for the joy of the Lord is your strength."

Isaiah 40:31 -But those who wait on the Lord Shall renew their strength; They shall mount up with wings like eagles, They shall run and not be weary, They shall walk and not faint.

From Sorrow to Singing

Psalm 42:11 -Why are you cast down, O my soul? And

why are you disquieted within me? Hope in God; For I shall yet praise Him, The help of my countenance and my God.

Psalm 126:2 -Then our mouth was filled with laughter, And our tongue with singing. Then they said among the nations, "The LORD has done great things for them."

Psalm 100:2 -Serve the Lord with gladness; Come before His presence with singing.

James 5:13 -Is anyone among you suffering? Let him pray. Is anyone cheerful? Let him sing psalms.

From Suffering to Survival

I Peter 4:19 -Therefore let those who suffer according to the will of God commit their souls to Him in doing good, as to a faithful Creator.

I Peter 3:17 -For it is better, if it is the will of God, to suffer for doing good than for doing evil.

I Timothy 2:12 -And I do not permit a woman to teach or to have authority over a man, but to be in silence.

Hebrews 11:25 -Choosing rather to suffer affliction with the people of God than to enjoy the passing pleasures of sin.

Psalm 34:4 -I sought the Lord, and He heard me, And delivered me from all my fears.

Psalm 119: 92 -Unless Your law had been my delight, I would then have perished in my affliction.

Deuteronomy 6:24 -And the Lord commanded us to observe all these statutes, to fear the Lord our God, for our good always, that He might preserve us alive, as it is this day.

From Struggle to Success

Ephesians 6:12 -For we do not wrestle against flesh and blood, but against principalities, against powers, against the rulers of the darkness of this age, against spiritual hosts of wickedness in the heavenly places.

Hebrews 10:32 -But recall the former days in which, after you were illuminated, you endured a great struggle with sufferings.

Genesis 24:40 -But he said to me, 'The Lord, before

whom I walk, will send His angel with you and prosper your way; and you shall take a wife for my son from my family and from my father's house.

Deuteronomy 29:9 -Therefore keep the words of this covenant, and do them, that you may prosper in all that you do.

From Trouble to Trust

Proverbs 12:13 -The wicked is ensnared by the transgression of his lips, But the righteous will come through trouble.

II Chronicles 15:4 -But when in their trouble they turned to the Lord God of Israel, and sought Him, He was found by them.

Psalm 86:7 -In the day of my trouble I will call upon You, For You will answer me.

Proverbs 3:5-6 -5 Trust in the Lord with all your heart, And lean not on your own understanding; 6 In all your ways acknowledge Him, And He shall direct your paths.

Psalm 20:7 -Some trust in chariots, and some in horses;

But we will remember the name of the Lord our God.

Psalm 118:8-9 -8 It is better to trust in the Lord Than to put confidence in man. 9 It is better to trust in the Lord Than to put confidence in princes.

From Tears to Thanksgiving

Psalm 126:5 -Those who sow in tears Shall reap in joy.

Revelation 21:4 -And God will wipe away every tear from their eyes; there shall be no more death, nor sorrow, nor crying. There shall be no more pain, for the former things have passed away.

Psalm 56:8 -You number my wanderings; Put my tears into Your bottle; Are they not in Your book?

Psalm 69:30 -I will praise the name of God with a song, And will magnify Him with thanksgiving.

Philippians 4:6 -Be anxious for nothing, but in everything by prayer and supplication, with thanksgiving, let your requests be made known to God;

Psalm 147:7 -Sing to the Lord with thanksgiving; Sing

praises on the harp to our God.

From Tragedy to Triumph

Hebrews 3:17-18 - 17 Now with whom was He angry forty years? Was it not with those who sinned, whose corpses fell in the wilderness? 18 And to whom did He swear that they would not enter His rest, but to those who did not obey?

Romans 8:28 -And we know that all things work together for good to those who love God, to those who are the called according to His purpose.

Psalm 30:5 -For His anger is but for a moment, His favor is for life; Weeping may endure for a night, But joy comes in the morning.

From Testing to Teaching

II Timothy 2:3 -You therefore must endure hardship as a good soldier of Jesus Christ.

I Peter 1:7 -That the genuineness of your faith, being much more precious than gold that perishes, though it is tested by fire, may be found to praise, honor, and glory at the revelation of Jesus Christ.

I Peter 4: 12-13 -12 Beloved, do not think it strange concerning the fiery trial which is to try you, as though some strange thing happened to you; 13 but rejoice to the extent that you partake of Christ's sufferings, that when His glory is revealed, you may also be glad with exceeding joy.

Psalm 144:1 -Blessed be the Lord my Rock, Who trains my hands for war, And my fingers for battle.

Matthew 5:19 -Whoever therefore breaks one of the least of these commandments, and teaches men so, shall be called least in the kingdom of heaven; but whoever does and teaches them, he shall be called great in the kingdom of heaven.

From Un-thankfulness to Understanding

Proverbs 16:18 -Pride goes before destruction, And a haughty spirit before a fall.

Philippians 2:14 -Do all things without complaining and

disputing.

Proverbs 1:5 -A wise man will hear and increase learning, And a man of understanding will attain wise counsel,

Proverbs 2:6 -For the Lord gives wisdom; From His mouth come knowledge and understanding.

Unity

Psalm 133:1 -Behold, how good and how pleasant it is For brethren to dwell together in unity!

Ecclesiastes 4:9 -Two are better than one, Because they have a good reward for their labor.

Ephesians 4:2-3 -2 With all lowliness and gentleness, with longsuffering, bearing with one another in love, 3 endeavoring to keep the unity of the Spirit in the bond of peace.

From Victim to Victory

Numbers 14:3 -Why has the Lord brought us to this land to fall by the sword, that our wives and children should become victims? Would it not be better for us to return to Egypt?"

I John 5:4 -For whatever is born of God overcomes the world. And this is the victory that has overcome the world our faith.

From Violence to Vow

Psalm 50:14 -Offer to God thanksgiving, And pay your vows to the Most High.

Ecclesiastes 5:4-5 -4 When you make a vow to God, do not delay to pay it; For He has no pleasure in fools. Pay what you have vowed. 5 Better not to vow than to vow and not pay.

Colossians 3:2 -Set your mind on things above, not on things on the earth.

Psalm 11:5 -The Lord tests the righteous, But the wicked and the one who loves violence His soul hates.

Proverbs 22:24 -Make no friendship with an angry man, And with a furious man do not go.

From Visual to Vision

Romans 4:20-21 -20 He did not waver at the promise of God through unbelief, but was strengthened in faith, giving glory to God, 21 and being fully convinced that what He had promised He was also able to perform.

Habakkuk 2:2-3 -2 Then the LORD answered me and said: "Write the vision And make it plain on tablets, That he may run who reads it. 3 For the vision is yet for an appointed time; But at the end it will speak, and it will not lie. Though it tarries, wait for it; Because it will surely come, It will not tarry.

Deuteronomy 28:7 -"The Lord will cause your enemies who rise against you to be defeated before your face; they shall come out against you one way and flee before you seven ways.

II Corinthians 12:9-10 -9 And He said to me, "My grace is sufficient for you, for My strength is made perfect in weakness." Therefore most gladly I will rather boast in my infirmities, that the power of Christ may rest upon me. 10 Therefore I take pleasure in infirmities, in reproaches, in needs, in persecutions, in distresses, for Christ's sake. For when I am weak, then I am strong.

From Weakness to Wisdom

Psalm 51:6 -Behold, You desire truth in the inward parts, And in the hidden part You will make me to know wisdom.

Psalm 90:12 -So teach us to number our days, that we may gain a heart of wisdom.

From Worry to Worship

Psalm 37:1 -Do not fret because of evildoers, Nor be envious of the workers of iniquity.

Psalm 29:2 -Give unto the Lord the glory due to His name; Worship the Lord in the beauty of holiness.

Psalm 149:1 -Praise the Lord! Sing to the Lord a new song, And His praise in the assembly of saints.

John 4:23-24 -But the hour is coming, and now is, when the true worshipers will worship the Father in spirit and truth; for the Father is seeking such to worship Him. 24 God is Spirit, and those who worship Him must worship in spirit and truth.

From X-ray to Xing to X-disease

Psalm 17:3-9-You have tested my heart; You have visited me in the night; You have tried me and have found nothing; I have purposed that my mouth shall not transgress. 4 Concerning the works of men, By the word of Your lips, I have kept away from the paths of the destroyer. 5 Uphold my steps in Your paths, that my footsteps may not slip. 6 I have called upon You, for You will hear me, O God; Incline Your ear to me, and hear my speech. 7 Show Your marvelous loving kindness by Your right hand, O You who save those who trust in You, From those who rise up against them. 8 Keep me as the apple of Your eye; Hide me under the shadow of Your wings, 9 From the wicked who oppress me, From my deadly enemies who surround me.

Psalm 139:23 -Search me, O God, and know my heart;

Try me, and know my anxieties;

Psalm 26:2 -Examine me, O Lord, and prove me; Try my mind and my heart.

From Yearning to Yielding

Philippians 3:7-8 -7 But what things were gain to me, these I have counted loss for Christ. 8 Yet indeed I also count all things loss for the excellence of the knowledge of Christ Jesus my Lord, for whom I have suffered the loss of all things, and count them as rubbish, that I may gain Christ.

Psalm 84:2 -My soul longs, yes, even faints. For the courts of the Lord; My heart and my flesh cry out for the living God.

Romans 6:13 -And do not present your members as instruments of unrighteousness to sin, but present yourself to God as being alive from the dead and your members as instruments of righteousness to God.

From Zeal to Zealous

Joshua 22:5 -But take careful heed to do the commandment and the law which Moses the servant of the Lord commanded you, to love the Lord your God, to walk in all His ways, to keep His commandments, to hold fast to Him, and to serve Him with all your heart and with all your soul.

Proverbs 22:29 -Do you see a man who excels in his work? He will stand before kings; He will not stand before unknown men.

Ecclesiastes 9:10 -Whatever your hand finds to do, do it with your might; for there is no work or device or knowledge or wisdom in the grave where you are going.

Romans 10:1-3 -1 Brethren, my heart's desire and prayer to God for Israel is that they may be saved. 2 For I bear them witness that they have a zeal for God, but not according to knowledge. 3 For they being ignorant of God's righteousness, and seeking to establish their own righteousness, have not submitted to the righteousness of God.

Scripture Notes

What scripture do you feel led to meditate on today?

_____

_____

_____

_____

_____

_____

_____

_____

What scripture do you feel led to meditate on today?

_____

_____

_____

_____

_____

_____

_____

_____

_____

What scripture do you feel led to meditate on today?

_____

_____

_____

_____

_____

_____

_____

_____

_____

_____

What scripture do you feel led to meditate on today?

_____

_____

_____

_____

_____

_____

_____

_____

_____

_____

What scripture do you feel led to meditate on today?

_____

_____

_____

_____

_____

_____

_____

_____

_____

_____

What scripture do you feel led to meditate on today?

_____

_____

_____

_____

_____

_____

_____

_____

_____

_____

What scripture do you feel led to meditate on today?

_____

_____

_____

_____

_____

_____

_____

_____

_____

What scripture do you feel led to meditate on today?

_____

_____

_____

_____

_____

_____

_____

_____

_____

What scripture do you feel led to meditate on today?

What scripture do you feel led to meditate on today?

I would like to take this time and extend an opportunity for you to accept Jesus as your personal Savior. If you are willing to pray the sinner's prayer with me, you can be saved right now while reading this journal. Please pray this prayer out loud:

Salvation Prayer

Heavenly Father, I pray this prayer as an act of belief to Romans 10:9 which says, *that if you confess with your mouth the Lord Jesus, and believe in your heart that God has raised Him from the dead, you will be saved.* In Jesus' Name, I repent of my sins and open my heart to let you come inside of me. I believe that You are the Lord Jesus Christ. Jesus, You are my Lord and Savior. I believe you died for my sins and you were raised from the dead. Cleanse me with your blood and fill me with Your Holy Spirit.

Thank you Father for saving me, in Jesus' Name, Amen.

Also by this Author

Against All Odds Book

A must read Miraculous Story

Available at:

www.thefaithchurchministries.com

www.amazon.com

www.barnesandnoble.com

Made in the USA
Charleston, SC
24 April 2013